D0419359

A city adventure in ...

New York

by Amy Allatson

Words in blue can be found in the glossary on page 24.

Contents

©2017
Book Life
King's Lynn
Norfolk PE30 4LS

ISBN: 978-1-78637-055-6

Written by:
Amy Allatson

Edited by:
Charlie Ogden

Designed by:
Ian McMullen

All rights reserved
Printed in Malaysia

A catalogue record for this book
is available from the British Library.

What is a City?

Cities are urban settlements. They are bigger in size than towns and villages and have larger populations. Cities are usually very busy places with lots of buildings.

In every country there are cities and most countries have a capital city. Cities are often home to people from many different cultures.

WHAT IS A CAPITAL CITY?
A capital city is usually home to a country's government.

Where is New York?

New York City, often just called New York, is is the biggest city in the United States of America (USA). It is located on the north-east coast of America around the Hudson River.

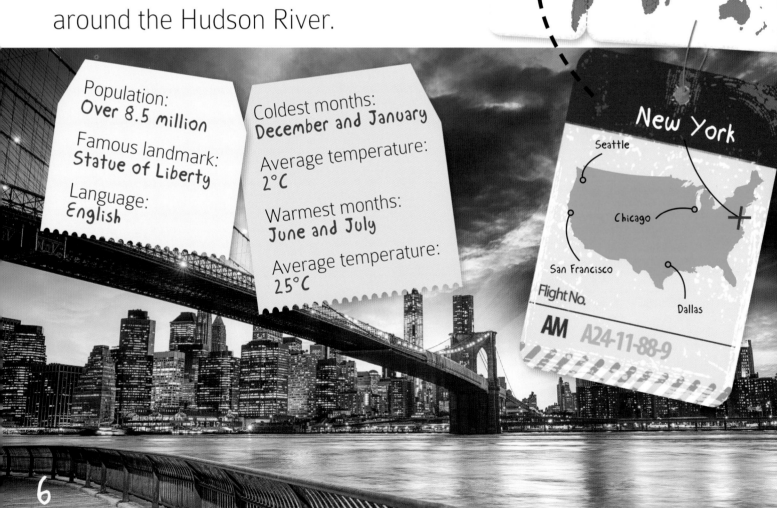

Population:
Over 8.5 million

Famous landmark:
Statue of Liberty

Language:
English

Coldest months:
December and January

Average temperature:
2°C

Warmest months:
June and July

Average temperature:
25°C

New York

Seattle

Chicago

San Francisco

Dallas

Flight No.

AM   A24-11-88-9

More people live in New York than any other city in the USA.
It has lots of tall buildings and tourist attractions and is often
called the 'Big Apple'.

Where and Why?

New York City began when a small number of people from Europe settled on one of the many islands that now make the city.

New York City used to be called New Amsterdam.

The city sits on a very large harbour known as New York Harbour. In the past it was used to trade items such as cotton, but today it is mostly used by cruise ships.

9

Sightseeing in New York

Statue of Liberty

There are many things to see and do in New York City. Tourists can visit the Statue of Liberty which is in the New York Harbour. The statue represents the American people's *freedom*.

The statue is 93 metres tall.

85998

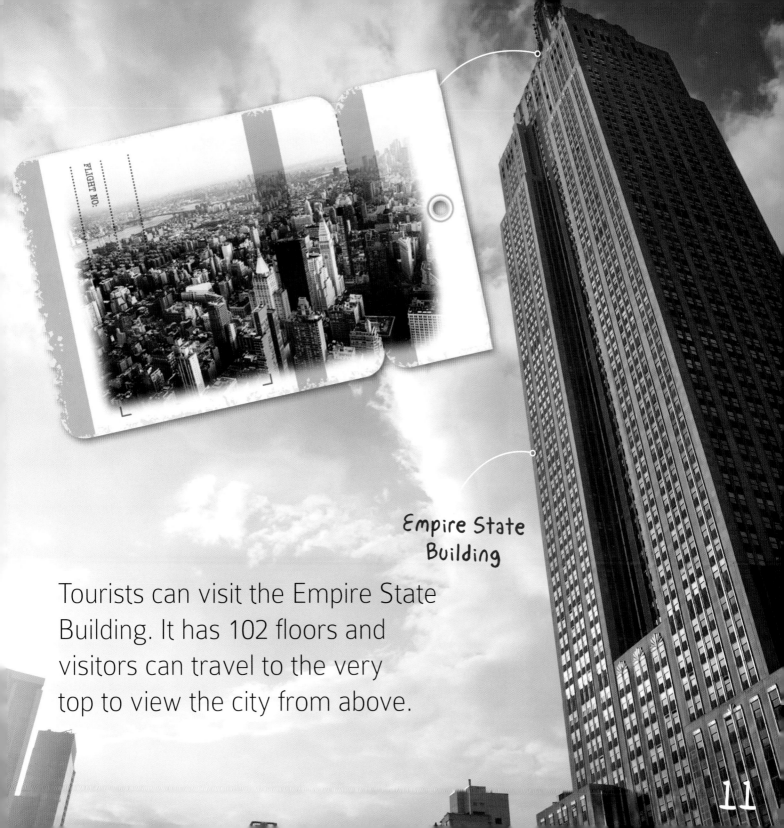

FLIGHT NO:

Empire State
Building

Tourists can visit the Empire State
Building. It has 102 floors and
visitors can travel to the very
top to view the city from above.

Food in New York

Italian food, such as pizza, is very popular in New York. This is because over the last 100 years many people from Italy have settled in the USA.

Pizza is traditionally cooked in a coal oven.

Bagels are also very common in New York City. They can be filled with cream cheese, salmon or salami.

Travelling Around New York

People often travel around New York City's busy streets in bright yellow taxis. These yellow taxis are famous around the world and very popular with tourists.

There are over 13,000 yellow taxis in New York City.

New York City's Subway

People also travel around New York City on a railway network called the Subway. The trains travel underneath the city at very high speeds.

Where do People Live in New York?

Lots of people who live in New York City live in *modern* flats in very tall buildings.

Other people live in buildings called townhouses. They usually have steep stairs leading up from the street and are sometimes painted bright colours.

Geography

New York City is built around New York Harbour. The harbour is one of the largest natural harbours in the world.

New York City is made up of over 35 islands, which are joined together by many bridges.

The main islands that make up New York City are Manhattan Island, Staten Island and Long Island.

Out and About

There are lots of things to do and see in New York. Many people like to visit a large park in the centre of the city, known as Central Park. There is a zoo in the park where people can see animals such as penguins and snow leopards.

FLIGHT NO:

In winter, when it is very cold and sometimes snowy, people can skate on the park's ice rink.

21

What is It?

Can you write down what's in the pictures below?

These are all things that are found in New York City.

Quick Quiz

1. How many people live in New York City?

2. Can you name a famous landmark in New York City?

3. What can you eat in New York City?

4. Where can you go to see animals in New York City?

5. How can you travel around New York City?

Glossary

cultures	attitudes and beliefs of a country or group of people
freedom	to be free
government	a group of people who make a country's rules and laws
harbour	a part of an ocean or lake that is next to land and is deep enough for ships
islands	areas of land surrounded by water
modern	something from present or recent times
populations	the number of people who live in certain places
railway network	connected railway tracks and stations
trade	to buy and sell goods
urban settlements	places where lots of people live and work, like towns or cities

Index

Photo Credits

Abbreviations: l-left, r-right, b-bottom, t-top, c-centre, m-middle.
Front Cover, 1, 24 – Zarya Maxim Alexandrovich. 2-3 – S.Borisov. 4 – CroMary. 5 – Zarya Maxim Alexandrovich 6, 15 – pisaphotography. 7 – Ollyy.
8 – Marzolino. 9 – ChameleonsEye. 9r – Skoda. 10 – NaughtyNut. 11 – Manuel Hurtado. 11t - Yulia Mayorova. 12 – kamira777. 13, 23 – Markus
Mainka. 14, 20 – Stuart Monk. 16 – Sean Pavone. 17 – rSnapshotPhotos. 18 – Samuel Acosta. 19 – ChameleonsEye. 20inset – Abeselom Zerit.
21 – Stuart Monk. 23tr – Dja65 23l – GulKar 23m – TRINACRIA PHOTO.
Images are courtesy of Shutterstock.com. With thanks to Getty Images, Thinkstock Photo and iStockphoto.